THE PEOPLE'S CHAMP

Carl Allen

THE PEOPLES' CHAMP
by Carl Allen
Published by One Faith Publishing
Richmond, VA, Port Huron, MI
onefaithpublishings@gmail.com

This book or parts thereof may not be reproduced in any form, stored in a retrieval system, or transmitted in any forms by any means -electronic, mechanical, photocopy, recording, or otherwise-written without written permission of the publisher and/or author, Carl Allen, except as provided by United States of America copyright law.

Unless otherwise, noted all Scripture quotations are from the King James Version (KJV) used by permission of public domain. 8 CPS TIPS provided by Vincent W. Davis & Associates.com (by use of public domain)

Copyright © 2022 by Carl Allen
All rights reserved.

Contents

Dedication 5
ACKNOWLEDGMENTS 6
Introduction 9
Chapter 1 11
   BACK IN THE DAY.. 11
CHAPTER 2 23
   MY POINT OF VIEW... 23
CHAPTER 3 25
   MY CASE... 25
Chapter 4 28
   PORT HURON.. 28
CHAPTER 5 30
   QUALIFIED IMMUNITY... 30
CHAPTER 6 32
   LAWS.. 32
Chapter 7 36
   BENCH TRIALS... 36
CHAPTER 8 38
   DO WE REALLY CARE?... 38
Chapter 9 40
   FAMILY COURT.. 40
Chapter 10 42
   8 CHILD PROTECTIVE SERVICES DEFENSE TIPS ... 42
CHAPTER 10 49
   WHO AM I?... 49

MY CHILDREN 52
WHAT'S YOUR STORY? 54

DEDICATION

The Peoples' Champ is dedicated to every parent who has committed suicide after the termination of their parental rights, and to the parents who held on and continuously prayed every night for your child's safety, happiness, and most importantly, that they will always remember you.

ACKNOWLEDGMENTS

To my children, Ebone, Jakari, Carl Jr., Maciahla, and Carrianna…You are my world, and I love you!

To my parents, Georgia and Delmus Allen, thank you for introducing me to God, by far, this is the greatest asset I've had in my life.

Tammy Jae Swafford, this is a dream come true. Without your vision and faith, I don't know how I would have done this without you. Thank you for believing in me and for seeing something I couldn't see within myself, and for knowing and seeing my passion for human rights. I know I may have been a hand full here and there but thank you for your patience…I love you!

To my sisters, Carla and Sharon, thank you for supporting me through your love and genuine conversations.

To my niece, Sade Coleman. I'm so proud of you for graduating from college, surely it is one, if not the greatest accomplishment in our family.

To my nieces, Martinique and Jameshia who calls Unk every day... lol

I love you, nieces

To my nephews, Charles, Meech, and Matt. The goal isn't to be like Uncle Carl, in fact, I'm proud of each one of you for being a stand-up gentleman. I love that put your children first and for walking in your individual light and not wanting to be like everyone else, yet you're boldly carving your own lanes in life.

I love you!

To Kevin Watkins (NAACP). Our organization will be faced with a lot of challenges; however, I do know that we are dedicated to truth and most importantly change. I look forward to working alongside all the members of the NAACP. Thank you!

To Momma Audrey (Zion Cathedral of Praise) on my worse days, you comforted me and always answered my phone calls no matter what time it was.

THANK YOU FOR BELIEVING in me!

To Pastor Kim Brown (ZCPIM) for your words of encouragement and faith in me. Forever I am grateful and very much humble.

To Mother Moore, I love your realness and how you invest in others, knowing that it may not always come back, but you do it from the kindness of your heart, and for that, you'll forever be blessed!

To my guys, Thomas. Roeskey Neal. Pooh, Greg, Tony, Valiant Hunt, and Sarah Cluesman for your support and coming to court for the kids, Andre Sasser, Setting Trendz (Big Kevin), and Grant & Nikki Long…Thank you all!

To my family and friends, I love you!

To the people that are still in their feelings about me… I love you too!

Shout Out To Chicago 79th N Woods and Sion Temple Church Of God In Christ!

A special shout out To Bread Of Life Baptist Church, Jubill Masonic Lodge 664, NAACP (the Port Huron Branch), and Zion Cathedral Of Praise International Ministries!

INTRODUCTION

Our land of opportunity and promise should be so heavily protected and guarded that our children shouldn't have to worry. They shouldn't worry about going to school and wondering if their school is going to be gunned down. Our children are trying to receive an education; therefore, schools should be locked down for their safety, playgrounds should be locked down, and social media accounts by minors should be more closely monitored by parents and adults.

Pastors, parental advocates, local administrators, community councils, congressman, and the State Senators House of Representatives should be protecting minors from trafficking and enforcing policies and procedures.

Family Services judges should be put under a microscope when implementing immunity in cases that decide if children and family should be split up, and the courts should not be allowed to win cases off perjury, corruption, and manipulation of documents.

A mass amount of children in the United States of America has been removed from their parents, not because of facts, but because of hearsay. This is a movement that financially generates billions off the backs of children, and very little of that money goes toward stabilizing the children. Instead, it goes to higher court entities, which is the same as prison investing.

As a community we should call upon our religious leaders to speak out on the day-to-day mistreatment of human life instead of cherry picking the headline news. To date, there are tons of stories in our neighborhoods that do not make it to the headliner of the news.

Question: Why isn't our religious leaders more upfront when someone in our community is murdered, abused, or neglected? This question may never be answered, or many of our communities' issues addressed and corrected, but as a voice for many, I will continue to do my part, and ***fight for parental rights.***

Chapter 1

BACK IN THE DAY...

Growing up in the '70s on the south side of Chicago, you had to be tough with an extra measure of thick skin or you weren't going to make it in that type of environment because the weak were seemingly preyed upon.

Every day it seemed like I had to contend with a bully, jokester, or prankster. Somedays I didn't know how I was going to make it through, but thankfully, I was blessed with some hardworking, devoted, and loving Christian parents.

At the same time, Mayor Jane Burn was our mayor before our first black Mayor Harold Washington was elected. Around 1984, Chicago's High School basketball prospect standout, and NBA-bound player, Ben Wilson was slain. It was a devastating shockwave that brought the city to its knees.

Nonetheless, I loved everything about the south side of Chicago because it made me who I am today, even my grade schools, Oglesby, Clara Barton, and Mahalia

Jackson played a major part in my development but like most kids, I was a pain in the butt, yet I cared about what my family thought about me. This meant, I was extra careful with avoiding a lot of trouble because of our religious beliefs; plus, I did not want to embarrass Delmus and Georgia Allen.

In the earlier years of my life, my mother was a life insurance agent, and she also managed a daycare before starting her own business, and my father was a Chicago transit bus driver and a part-time coach driver. Therefore, those examples of being a positive person were installed in me the very moment they adopted and graciously accepted me into their home, but life before my adoption is a different story.

My sister and I were born two months premature, and we were diagnosed with Fetal Alcohol Syndrome. With that being said, the doctors immediately labeled us as Mildly Retarded with Low Independent Living Skills. Shortly after birth, we were separated and placed in foster care, and as far back as I can remember, I was tossed between four different foster homes before I was legally adopted around 5 years old.

After the adoption was finalized, I got a second chance to be reconnected with my twin sister. Our adopted families agreed that we should have regular communication with each other. As a foster child, I have seen my share of a broken system, but thanks to my sister,

I learned a lot about who I am as an individual due to our consistent communication.

No, our relationship wasn't as good as it could have been because when you hear shady stories of how family members treat or harm their own, it makes you think twice about bonding. Still, it never crossed our minds to demean or physically harm each other.

Yes, we argued, but we also gave each other the space and time that was needed to calm down. I believe those values were instilled in us since we both grew up in loving homes. We had foster parents who cared enough to allow my sister and I to see each other as often as possible. But even though my sister was there, I still felt that something deeper was missing from my life.

After my sister and I were given a few details about our adoption, we often talked about what it would be like if we ever met our biological parents. There was plenty of days when I sat alone and wondered what it would be like to be around my biological family or if there were any resemblance.

Daily I yearned for an opportunity to stare at my biological mother's picture and her face, but that day never came. Instead, my sister became my strength, which helped me to gain a better understanding at a young age of everything that was taking place in our lives.

Even though I never knew the full story or the underlying conditions that placed us in foster care, and whatever I did know was through a third party...my adoptive parents. Yet, I was eagerly open to knowing my biological parents. During that time, it didn't matter what they did or did not do because my heart was in a no-judgment zone due to being raised in a Christian home.

Regardless of the circumstances, I knew firsthand that I couldn't judge them or anyone else, and since I didn't know the real reasons why I was placed in foster care, how could I judge? But what I did know is that I wanted to forgive my mother so I could move on with my life, still, a part of me desired to know about the family I originated from. I wanted to be a part of the 80% percentile of foster kids who still love and respected their biological parents. Yet, it seemed like a lost cause, so for a long time I mentally swayed away from dealing with the fact that I had a family outside of my adoptive family.

Growing up in an adopted household, I genuinely wanted to be accepted and loved as a youngster. Thankfully, I was adopted into a large family with quite a few cousins on both sides of my parents, but most didn't know that I was adopted. As for the ones who knew, they made a point of reminding me that I was adopted every chance they got, but for the most part, I was treated well.

There were plenty of days when I rebelled against my adoptive parents; the reason being, I didn't know much about my them, and I felt as if they were not open to me knowing who my biological parents were. I didn't understand that they were being protective because they felt that my biological parents were the reason I came into their care in the first place.

Around that same time of my issues, my twin sister was also having issues about being alienated by her adopted family, but the most important trait I learned through it all was…faith.

When I was about 8 years old, I was nonverbal due to the trauma of my biological mom, from being bounced from foster home to foster home, and for being left in the care of a sick elderly man who passed away while my sister and I were still in the home. So, yes, the combination of those different traumas played a part in my mental awareness.

The doctors said I wouldn't grow out of having severe head tremors but one day my adoptive parent's prayers were answered, and by age eleven I had beaten most of the medical odds that were against me. Thankfully, my adoptive parents kept me involved and active with other "normal" children to help me with living a healthy lifestyle, but most importantly, they believed in a higher spiritual power, and they consistently prayed for me.

My adopted mother was deeply involved in the church, she was the organist and the choir director for both the youth and young adults, which meant, I was also deeply involved by going to church at least four times a week. Because of my upbringing, I learned early on that having a faith-based religion is essential.

Unfortunately, religion is not a guaranteed way to rid oneself of trouble, however, my friends who were growing up in church didn't seem to get into a lot of drama or trouble compared to my friends who didn't frequently go to church.

They say opposites attract, so even though I was raised in the church, I was physically drawn to the streets. I soaked up street conversations and stories, and I watched the way boys my age carried themselves because I wanted to duplicate their lifestyle and behavior. For me, it was more exciting to be exposed to kids that lived different lifestyles. It was a lifestyle that I craved and before I knew it, I was living a double life.

Still, I had to be smart because I didn't want my parents to find out, so I used my love for basketball and the court. I used my basketball court time to keep up with the current affairs in the streets.

In the 80s and 90s, many moms were either nurses or housekeepers, and the men worked for the Chicago Transit or Ford Automotive. Both of my parents worked but that didn't keep us out of the government cheese care package line on Saturdays.

This was all during the button era, as I like to call it because buttons were everywhere. There were Michael Jackson buttons, Harold Washington buttons, and Prince buttons that seemed to be worn by everyone in Chicago. This was also at a time when I had friends who were deep into the street life.

I had this one friend who basically raised himself, and we would meet up every day before school or at the Hermitage Candy Store (that's where all the kids went before school to get their candy for the day), and by the time I reached 7th grade there was very little that I didn't know about the streets.

It didn't take long before I was labeled as the class clown, and that meant, I was under constant surveillance by the teachers. principal, and staff. Therefore, I had to give my friends my candy to hold for me, and throughout the day whenever I changed classes I would have a piece of candy passed to me while en route.

I loved school, and I also loved riding the bus and eating lunch because it allowed me more time to spend with my sister. I don't believe foster parents, or the courts fully understand what happens when children are separated by Family Court. It's important to understand that the children need to maintain consistent communication with their siblings because it is overall healthy for the children's mental, physical, and emotional development.

Even though I loved school, and I could easily comprehend reading, writing, spelling, and physical education, I had a major problem with math. It seemed to be all mumble jumbled together with symbols that seemed to close in on me. It was overwhelming, and in my young mind, I just couldn't get it. I even tried to tell the time, but it was just as difficult as the math problems.

It was hard for my adopted mom to sit hour after hour, just for me to forget some of the topics we covered minutes before. Out of her frustration, she responded by saying, you're slow, stupid, or retarded. Hearing my mom's frustration and disappointment made me feel different about myself, and because I heard those words so much, I internally began to believe that maybe I was retarded. Eventually, I was placed in an L.D. class (Learning Disability). I went from a class size of 25 kids down to a class filled with about 6 kids, including me.

The change of class caused my friends to tease me, but to avoid the teasing I'd say that I was a room monitor or an aid to the school bus driver. At the same time, my sister and placed in special education classes which stemmed from our biological mother's alcohol abuse.

As a result, we suffered from issues that are associated with Fetal Alcohol Syndrome, meanwhile, the doctors and educators ruled us out from having an ordinary life, and for the most part, they were right. As I was going through this troubling time, my mom told me something one day that was enriched and profound, she said, "Carl, your special, which means, you don't have to try and be like the other kids. All you have to do is go at your own pace." and from that day forward, I did things differently and within my own pace.

I've always wanted to write and be comical because being funny was my defense when kids laughed and talked about me. Back in the day we called it "the dozens or capping" it's when you joked around at the lunchroom table talking about each other or our parents, even our mommas and daddies weren't off limits.

Being a comedian was something I was good at, even though I was about 5'4, chubby, and I wore some of the thickest glasses probably ever recorded to man. My glasses were so thick that a bully smacked my glasses off my face so hard that they landed about 10 feet away and they still didn't break.

Due to my parents being constant churchgoers, teaching me to fight was out of the question, so if I was approached by some kids who wanted to fight, I'd run like hell nonstop until I reached home. After the incident with my glasses, I was never touched or caught, therefore I gained the reputation as being the fastest runner in my neighborhood. I got so good at running, that if my parents didn't have lunch money for that day, I would race for a dollar.

Instantly, I went from being called, blind ass and four eyes to being named, Quick. I didn't care what I was called as long as it wasn't mean because I desired to be something other than what I was labeled.

As my mind matured, I struggled with the idea of when I die, am I to be buried under my biological name or my adoptive name? I also felt that if I had children, it would be less confusing to them if I left behind some sort of biological and adoption blueprint. This way there wouldn't be much confusion about my life as to where I initially evolved from.

From childhood to adulthood, I struggled with those thoughts and assumptions until I finally let them go. I was tired of going back and forth between the two and it was time for me to focus on where I was and those who genuinely loved and surrounded me.

Fortunately, I had cousins on my adoptive parent's side that never treated me bad or different, as well as my twin sister Carla, who always looked out for me whether we were in Garfield Elementary School, riding the school bus together, or passing each other in the halls at Percy L. Julian high school.

By the age of 19, I had transformed from a short 5`4 image to a 5`10 senior who began shedding his old nerdy dorky look into a handsome and chiseled young man. A young man who became curious about girls, cars, and intellectual conversations. Yet, I still had a lot of mastering to master, so I hung around people who were older and those who my mother trusted, like my older cousins. They taught me how to move and carry myself in the streets and church.

Ever since I was a child, establishing a one-on-one relationship with our Creator has always been implemented in my life, along with a scripture that followed me since my Sunday school days, Proverbs 3:6, *"In all thy ways acknowledge Him and He shall direct thy path."*

In short, this scripture means no matter what's going on in your life, God will guide you through it, but only if you trust in Him to do the unthinkable in your life. I'm forever grateful for the instilling of God over everything. No, I haven't always made the best decisions in my life, but throughout those bad decisions God has never left my side and He is still next to me today.

I don't think I was a bad child or ultimately a bad person due to my spiritual upbringing because my spiritual structure was the greatest thing that my adoptive parents have given me. I notice that people who believe in a higher power have a seemingly undisturbed inner peace, so I highly recommend for parents to implement God in their children's lives at an early age… it unquestionably can't hurt.

CHAPTER 2

MY POINT OF VIEW...

The foster parents in the 70s seemed to be more genuine in the development of their adopted children. The foster parents of today seem to be entranced with state and county payments, when in all actuality, it has been proven to be cheaper to keep a struggling household together. Instead, the system rather mirror the images of a slave owner's tactics by systemically breaking up households.

From my point of view, the structure of the adoption system looks similar to the slave trade. It was a system where parents were auctioned to plantation owners and colored children were sold to white households, all for profit.

We're in the 21st century and "all for profit" is still in full effect, meaning, the family court system has an annual revenue of millions, if not billions of dollars. This family court is designed to remove children from their parents by using a system most parents cannot win against.

This is an unjustified system where judges typically hide behind immunity, which allows them to use corruption and perjury against a parent which violates all parental rights. The Supreme Court suggests that parents should be able to freely parent their children without any intrusion from the lower courts or Children Protective Services. They also suggest that the court system should not interfere with a parent raising their children.

Sadly, the upper court values aren't upheld in the lower courts; therefore, it's much easier for the upper court to overlook any truths that pertain to a parent's case for removal or termination. Unfortunately, in these types of cases, everyone except the parent is benefitting one way or another.

I have often asked myself, where are all the adopted children who are now adults, and why aren't they speaking out? Why is there so many silent on an issue that involves our innocent children?

I believe the real National Monument should be a display of our children instead of the faces of dead presidents on a mountain. There should be a family court museums that document and display pictures and brief stories of every parent that has had their children removed by family court.

CHAPTER 3

MY CASE...

The odds were against me from the start because the judge had a history with my children's mother before she and I met. Yet, I still presented evidence that upheld my side and point of view, which made the judge even more determined to ignore the facts and implement his own opinion. Unfortunately, it was an opinion that wasn't based on facts.

As I mentioned earlier, my ex had a history of her children being removed from the home prior to me knowing her. After we separated, I was notified that due to her drug abuse, she was leaving our children with strangers. A reoccurring incident which caused Family Court and CPS to open a case against her.

Once I received the call, I left Chicago and moved back to Michigan. My sisters didn't want me to return to Michigan, but they also understood that I had to fight for my babies CJ, Carianna, and Macihla Allen, who were my main priority. In my mind, I knew this would be my greatest fight, but it was also a fight I was willing to give my life for.

In my case, it was shown that the family court used perjury, corruption, and falsification of documents. In fact, the judge's secretary was reprimanded for not presenting documents in a timely manner. There were also agents who sat on the stand and lied under oath and the judge allowed it. Throughout my case, I had to fire several attorneys for ineffective assistance.

Yes, I experienced corruption and, perjury in my case from,

1. An ineffective counsel
2. Corrupted state workers
3. A judge who allowed perjury

Those three powers together make it almost impossible to have a fair trial in the United States because they hide behind immunity. The court system is basically set up to believe hearsay over factual evidence, and we can't get justice, even when the facts are staring the prosecution, judge, and jury right in the face.

Sadly, in the State of Michigan there aren't any grandparents' or fathers' rights, so if a mom is somehow deemed incompetent to take care of her children the courts step in. With its designed fashion, the courts pretend to reunify families, but the sole underlying plan is to adopt immediately.

As I look back, I realized some of the mistakes I made from not having knowledge. My first major mistake was making contact with cps and the police officer who accompanied them. Sidenote: If cps shows up at your house without a warrant, do not open the door! Without a warrant, you do not have to open your door. Instead, tell them to get a warrant, and do not engage with them at all.

To date, there hasn't been much improvement by Child Protective Service to successfully unify parents with their children which is saddening. I send out a special prayer to the families separated by family court, just know that my heart is with you.

Chapter 4

PORT HURON...

I live in Port Huron, Michigan, it's basically a family ran small town but it's rapidly growing. This town has beautiful blue waters, and it is also one of the top attraction spots in Michigan. In the summer months the crystal blue waters and large ships sailing under the Canadian Bridge attracts people from all over the world, yet there's a dark cloud that continuously glooms over Port Huron.

I believe that dark cloud resides because of Albert Martin, a young black man who was lynched on the 7th Street bridge. Martin allegedly assaulted a white woman in 1889. He was arrested, but soon after his arrest, some "masked men" dragged him three blocks from a holding cell. He was already near death from the dragging and beating before a rope was tightened around his neck. To this day, there were no charges or arrests in Martin's death, not even a memorial in his honor, in fact, Martin's death seems to be erased from Port Huron's history.

From my understanding, there has never been a "safe zone" for blacks in Port Huron, beginning with the never mentioned underground railroad that hasn't been properly acknowledged for the slaves who risked their lives on the "Road to Freedom" from Port Huron to Canada. Let me not forget the blatant refusal to observe Dr. Martin Luther King's holiday in their public schools, which means, Port Huron schools are closed on every holiday except on MLK day.

If one was to closely observe, there are no black judges or attorneys, a very low percentage of black-owned businesses, some interracial relationship and friendships are taunted by white family members for having an association with blacks, and last but not least, Port Huron has a higher child removal rate than its larger cities such as Detroit, which is only 50 miles away.

Well, you may be wondering if Port Huron is that bad, why stay? I stay because there is a need for our voices to be heard, and once we are heard, then we can attempt to make a change.

CHAPTER 5

QUALIFIED IMMUNITY...

Parents all around this country have been affected one way or another, but more so in low-income neighborhoods. This is why my passion is to educate parents and to help them understand, that they too have rights. These rights are backed by the Supreme Court, even though the lower courts do not honor the higher courts instructions, and unfortunately, those that disregard these rights are covered by immunity.

This same immunity is used to keep judges, attorneys, CPS, and Family Court Agents protected, regardless of perjury, manipulative paperwork, or lying under oath. But until that day comes and immunity is removed from our court system, nothing will change.

To date, there are too many children being abused by foster parents, and there are too many biological parents that have been falsely accused. But in all fairness, there are some good foster parents who's overshadowed by the bad press, and unfortunately the bad parents make media headlines, but the good parents are often forgotten.

I pray that all those cases involved with qualified immunity be reviewed by some type of Innocence Project.

I believe parents should be allowed to file a Federal Class Action lawsuit against Family Court as well as CPS, both should be ultimately abolished after being defunded.

CHAPTER 6

LAWS...

On November 19, 1997, Bill Clinton signed, "The Adoption and Safe Families Act" this act allowed family courts worldwide to go after every child possible. The Act was seemly created to improve the safety of children and to promote adoption and other permanent homes for children. However, the primary purpose of the law was to shorter the length of time a child spends in foster care and speed up the process of freeing children for adoption.

In my opinion, I believe the sole mission of this law is to divide families and permanently separate children from their biological parents. Sadly, it's a law against climbing the National Monument and a law to protect a bald eagle, but why can't our children from state to state be protected?

In fact, these laws are held to a higher degree, to the point that if a bald eagle is harmed in any way, it's a felony, and to protect Mt Rushmore, it's illegal to climb this mountain. My question is, why can't our children from state to state be protected?

Nevertheless, I guess the most important question that any parents who have encountered family court or cps want to know...If the judges are telling the truth, why do they need immunity? It's simple, the judges allow lies, manipulation of programming, altered and manipulated documents, as well as perjury. This injustice is allowed to take away a parent's parental rights because they know that our children are the greatest assets in life.

As a black man in America, I am aware of two constitutions, the first is solely and strictly designed for whites, and the second constitution talks about the promise of land. This land was supposed to be given to blacks, but the Court of Appeals overturned that decision and said that they were not giving black people anything after slavery; so, for survival, many slaves were split in their decision-making to leave the plantation or stay after being freed.

Many felt that they would be better off staying with their masters, but on the other hand, many chose to battle nature's elements and scavenge, rather than deal with the continuous mistreatment by slave owners.

Of course, America as we know it needs to be changed, blacks should be entitled to reparations because they fought in this country's wars, they helped to build this country's railroads, and they have made great strides and contributions to medical science and inventions. Yet, we are still systemically oppressed by the lack of jobs in our communities.

There's absolutely no way a college graduate with a degree should be working in a fast-food restaurant. I believe a college graduate should walk straight into corporate America instead of straight into a restaurant or factory for work. But why is that? Especially when the United States is the wealthiest country on earth; yet we seem to systemically enslave our own citizens more than any third-world country.

Sadly, our country doesn't offer the help the citizens require and deserve. Listen, no veteran should ever be homeless, and anyone who has served in the United States Army, Navy Air Force, or the Marine shouldn't automatically have free housing, and if not free housing, then housing on a military base. That's the least that should be done for the veterans who have fought for this country.

Lastly, but definitely not least, abolish student loans and replace liquor stores in our communities with resource centers that will help and empower our generations to come, doing so, we help to have a more productive universal society for the future to come.

Chapter 7

BENCH TRIALS...

Here's the truth about bench trials, they are typically biased and 80 percent of the time they are in favor of the state judges, which again, allows perjury and manipulation of documents. Nearly all cases represented by bench trial judges have some sort of corruption or perjury involved.

After all, the judges have the last word, which means, the crimes of corruption and perjury in bench trials go untouched because the judges can hide their deeds of falsification of documents and mischief behind immunity.

The phrase, "Under the Penalty of Perjury" scares attorneys and state workers. This is a phrase a judge tries to avoid or refuses to touch. WHY? Because it holds them accountable for all their courtroom lies and corruption, and if presented to them before the representation, this phrase will generally let you if they will represent you truthfully and effectively.

Last, but not least, there's court-appointed attorneys who pretends to be in your corner, but their true intentions are focused on making a living. These attorneys' duty is solely to make the judge happy, which allows them to win future cases in that same judge's courtroom. I believe every case which involved a bench trial should be revisited and examined for violation of policy and procedure and ethical misconduct for abuse of power.

CHAPTER 8

DO WE REALLY CARE?...

Oftentimes, we turn away from the cries of a child to only respond with the excuse, "As long as it's not my child or anyone I know." But why should we care any less? If a child is being displaced or abused, I could give a dam about that child's original origin or relation.

Foster children are often brainwashed about their biological families, while foster parents are manipulated into changing the biological name of a foster child. I believe a name change further punishes the biological parents so they cannot easily find their children.

As an adult, you know how it feels to be unable to locate your children because the state has changed their name and social security number. You're searching for your sweet little Annie, not knowing the agency has changed your child's identity.

As a child, can you imagine being called and answering to a name for twelve years of your life, and one day you wake up in a new house, a new family, and with a new name? A new name that also erases a part of the child's identity of who they are.

What good parent wouldn't fight for their kids? But to be real, there are some bad circumstances where the biological parents should have been helped first. Instead, the parents are forever punished by having their kids removed and placed in an unrelated environment against the parent's will.

My proposal would consist of a board of adult adopted parents (who have been in foster care themselves) to assist in determining if Family Court and CPS followed protocol, policies, and procedures when attempting to remove children from their biological parents. My question to Family Court is, is it possible to remove a child from its biological family without implementing lies?

Chapter 9

FAMILY COURT...

I believe family court needs to be abolished because it's about secretly displacing and trafficking children right in the public's eye. The system's deceptive ways often blame parents without factual and supporting documentation such as hospital and police reports. This is why many parents wonder if it's possible to win against a corrupt system, and this thought alone keeps a lot of parents afraid of fighting back.

Also, there are too many parents that don't know how to fight back even if they wanted to. For this reason, some parents have committed suicide because they saw no hope.

300 River Place, Suite 5600
Detroit, Michigan 48207

(313) 283-0950
steven@stevenhelton.com

St. Clair County
Department of Health and Human Services
220 Fort St.
Port Huron, Michigan 48060

May 5, 2019

Re: Carl Allen

To Whom It May Concern:

I was appellate counsel to Carl Allen in *People v Allen*, Case. No. L-001942-FH.

In my representation of Mr. Allen, I reviewed all transcripts and pleadings in the above captioned case. I saw no allegation that Mr. Allen had ever abused or neglected any of his children. In fact, Mr. Allen's primary concern throughout the time that I have known him has been reunifying with his children. So much so, that when I was representing him he was willing to take actions that would place his own personal freedom at risk in hopes of increasing the likelihood that he would be reunited with his children.

Since my representation of Mr. Allen ended, he has often called me to keep me apprised of his ongoing efforts to regain custody of his children. I am in awe of the lengths he has gone to in order to achieve this goal, and his love of his children always comes through.

I am aware of no reason why Mr. Allen should not be reunified with his children. I believe that Mr. Allen is a loving parent and would be a responsible and caring guardian to his children.

Sincerely,

/s/Steven Helton
Steven Helton

Chapter 10

8 CHILD PROTECTIVE SERVICES DEFENSE TIPS

Why is the Fourth Amendment often cited in Child Protective Services cases?

The Fourth Amendment states, "The right of the people to be secure in their persons, houses, papers, and effects, against unreasonable searches and seizures, shall not be violated, and no Warrants shall issue, but upon probable cause, supported by Oath or affirmation, and particularly describing the place to be searched, and the persons or things to be seized."

Below are 8 Tips on how to handle a CPS social worker or police officer at your door who are investigating allegations of child abuse or child neglect.

1. If you are phoned or contacted in person by a CPS or DCFS Social Worker and told that there is an allegation made against you, inquire

with the social worker the exact nature of the complaint against you.

Furthermore, request them to give you the actual state statute number or local ordinance code that you have allegedly violated. Write it down. If you are surprised at your door, and don't have a pen and paper, politely ask their forgiveness while you gather writing material, excuse yourself for "a minute" calmly close, and quietly lock the door (don't be obvious), and go get something to write on. Return and make precise notes.

2. Identify the social worker(s) and/or police officer(s)persons at your door. Ask them for their business card(s) and write down their badge numbers. You already have your pen and paper at this point.

3. If you have advanced notice or suspect that you are being investigated and expect a home visit you might be able to document the front door or in-home conversation with a video camera or audio tape recorder. It is not unlawful to conceal the camera or recorder so that the social worker or police officer is unaware of the taping.

Many parents use such devices to protect their children from abuse from babysitters. This type of recording on your own property is never illegal, no matter what you are told by the social worker or police officer.

In California it is illegal to record a telephone call without the consent of **all parties to the conversation**. Penal Code § 632. That said, if you were to video tape yourself while talking on the phone so that your side of the conversation was recorded that might be useful to remember exactly what you said.

> 4. If the CPS / DCFS Social Worker asks to come into your home politely inform them that you'd rather not have them in. If they insist, coerce, or threaten you with some consequence for keeping them out, stand your ground.

If they persist ask the social worker or police officer if they have a warrant or court order that gives them the authority to enter your home against your will. If the social worker or police officer insists that they do not need a warrant under the circumstances, tell them again that you will be glad to cooperate and allow them to enter your home if they possess a warrant or court order signed by a judge or magistrate.

If a police officer then demands that you step out of the way and insists they are entering your home, it would be advisable to step aside or you might end up arrested. The abuse of authority can be addressed later without you ending up in a jail cell.

When can the police legally enter my home without a warrant? – Under limited circumstances, called **"exigent circumstances,**" "such as "in hot pursuit" and "emergency," police officers are legally permitted to enter a home without a warrant, but these instances are usually rare.

An example of "hot pursuit" and the legal authority to enter a private residence is sometimes seen by millions of people watching a televised police pursuit, as commonly seen here in Southern California, where the person crashes the car and then breaks into a close-by home or apartment.

The officers can enter that home without a warrant. An "emergency" would involve the "immediate need" to rescue someone from serious bodily harm. An officer hearing screaming, pleas for help, or gunshots coming from inside a home would perceive an "emergency," and would be justified in entering the home without a warrant. A social worker investigating allegations of child abuse or neglect –especially from an anonymous tip– would rarely be exempt from the legal requirement to have a warrant.

5. These same legal rights protect you should an officer of the court such as a CPS/DCFS social worker, or police officer attempt to convince or coerce you to do anything against your will. For example, you should not assume that you HAVE TO drive to and show up at the offices of the county social worker; nor should you be coerced to "bring your children into the CPS or DCFS offices to be interviewed" without being served with a legal court order to do so. Only a judge or magistrate, presented with evidence that you have committed a crime, can issue an

order that you are obligated to obey or comply with.

6. Unfortunately, 90% of people will mistakenly comply with such "orders" as they seem "mandatory" – all the while the CPS social workers are building a case against you with your help and your willing cooperation. If such requests are being made of you it might be time to seek legal counsel as it is likely that the social workers are, in fact, building a case against you.

If the CPS social worker or police officer uses force to enter your home against your will, it is in your best interest to NOT RESIST. Even if the forced entry into your home is unwarranted, you should not physically resist the officer of the court. Instead, advise the social worker or police officer that they do not have your permission to enter, and that if they continue entry into your home without your permission, you will pursue legal action against them.

If you were clued in that this visit was coming and the forced intrusion were recorded on a video or sound recorder, such evidence would be very helpful for your attorney and very helpful for you and your kids.

7. Attempt to record all of your telephone conversations with any CPS or DCFS employees. Recording devices for standard phones can be found at Radio Shack. For Smart

Phones, there are APPs available to record the calls, you can even place calls using your computer with Skype and use Skype recorders such as found HERE or HERE.

In California, it is unlawful to record a telephone conversation without the consent of both parties. Therefore, before continuing with the conversation ask the CPS social worker if he or she agrees that you record the call.

If they refuse, and you absolutely feel compelled to talk to social workers by phone, you could use your smart phone, tape recorder or video camera to record only your side of the conversation which might be useful for your attorney later on if the social workers actually end up taking your child/children from you.

As for being interviewed by the police, we would strongly advise that you **NEVER AGREE TO BE INTERVIEWED BY THE POLICE without a lawyer present**, nor speak with any police investigators by phone nor in person if you are being investigated or accused of any crime – no matter how minor they may suggest the crime is. The police have a job requirement to build a case and that's what you will help them do – no matter how innocent you might be. When the police are investigating you ALWAYS GET A LAWYER. Period!

8. Compile a list of emergency telephone numbers that will be readily accessible to you should any confrontation with a CPS / DCFS

social worker or police over the raising of your children, the discipline of your children, or any abuse or neglect of your children. In addition to a written list, take a few minutes and program these emergency phone numbers into your cell phone as Speed Dial Numbers.

For example: your spouse's work number, a neighbor who is on your side and would be willing (ahead of time) to come over and witness the interaction of you and the social worker, and a Juvenile Dependency and Criminal Defense lawyer who will be immediately available if your children are forcibly taken from you; if your children are taken from their school without your knowledge, or should you be arrested by the police.

CHAPTER 10

WHO AM I?...

Here's a tidbit about who I am... I became an advocate for parental rights because of my separation from my biological mom, and over the years I've watched many other children be torn away from their families. This traumatizing experience was enough to make me want to do something to help. It's just that simple, most parents who have lived this nightmare along with me can understand my frustration and disappointment.

Throughout my time of advocating, I have personally seen parents affected by systemic oppression by the monsters who represent themselves as family court. It's a system that pretends to represent parents and children state actors better known as children and family service workers all three have combined to implement hearsay.

I grew up in the system, but I was determined to not let the system make me bitter, resentful, or grumpy toward life. So, when I began fighting against the State of Michigan for my kids and children abroad, it essentially was a small thing to a giant like me. My determination pushed me to be the first in my family to fight from the Lower Court Civil (Port Huron, MI), to appealing in the US Courts of Appeal (Detroit), and appealing to the US Supreme Court (Washington DC)

Yes, I talk a lot about Family Court rights due to my personal experiences, nevertheless, I'm just a small add-on to a monstrous epidemic that is affecting White, Hispanic, and African Americans nationwide. There is a globally increasing number of families being affected worldwide by the family court at a phenomenal rate. Unfortunately, it's an ongoing antic that's been repeated upon African Americans since slavery, this is why equality and truth mean so much to me.

During my years of advocating, I've seen too many fathers give up, but I wasn't going to be one of them. I strived to be a father and no matter what came at me, I was going to stand tall through it all without giving up. Yes, life gets bumpy, but quitting should never be an option when you're fighting for love, the purest human form of love… our children.

To all the parents who have passed during your fight against family court, your fight wasn't in vain. Today, I carry in my heart the same passion and drive you willed to me, now it's in my spirit to fight for equality and targeted low-income citizens of Port Huron, Michigan, and abroad.

Today, I stand in representation to millions of adoptive adults and children. I feel it's time for a change, a change in the way we treat the parents and children in America. Ultimately, I won the fight for my children, and I will continue this fight for others. signed…..***The Peoples' Champ***

MY CHILDREN

A *Father* THINKS ABOUT HIS *Children* DAY AND NIGHT, EVEN WHEN THEY ARE NOT WITH HIM AND HE WILL LOVE THEM FOREVER IN A WAY THEY COULD NEVER UNDERSTAND.

WHAT'S YOUR STORY?

www.ingramcontent.com/pod-product-compliance
Lightning Source LLC
Chambersburg PA
CBHW071139090426
42736CB00012B/2172